Trebah

Adrian Poole

Introduction David White

First published 2014
Published by Truran
Truran is an imprint of Tor Mark,
United Downs Ind. Est., St Day,
Redruth TR16 5HY

Introduction © David White

Picture credits: all pictures © Adrian Poole
(except "Winter" © Chris Smale)

ISBN 978 185022 246 0

Designed by Alix Wood www.alixwood.co.uk

Printed by BoothsPrint, The Praze, Penryn,
Cornwall TR10 8AA

I should like to acknowledge the following for their
invaluable assistance:

Dr David White	- for inspiring me to produce this book
Darren Dickey	- Head Gardener Trebah
Nicola Wharton	- Trebah Archivist
Melanie Mallett	- Gallery Shop Manager
Nigel Burnett	- Trebah's Director
Ivan Corbett	- Publisher for Truran Books

The Trustees of Trebah Garden

Welcome to Trebah

The transformation of Trebah from wooded valley into the beautiful garden seen today owes much to the vision and effort of Charles Fox who bought the estate and Polgwiddon Cove in 1838. The steep-sided, narrow valley, south-facing and sheltered from cold easterly winds, is watered predominantly by warm wet south-westerly winds from the Atlantic Ocean. The relatively warm waters of the Gulf Stream wash the tidal shore of secluded Polgwiddon Cove on the scenic Helford River, an unspoiled estuary lined with ancient oak trees. Such conditions are conducive to a virtually frost-free environment and conspire to support the growth of species of flowers, plants and trees from more temperate regions of the world; they unite to form a special sense of place that is Trebah which the four miles of footpath enable the visitor to explore.

Trebah (from the Cornish 'house on or near the bay') has been settled for almost a thousand years and ownership of the land held by a number of Cornish families including the Killigrews of Falmouth. It was bought for almost five thousand pounds by Charles Fox, a member of the famous, philanthropic Quaker family, from the Nicholls family and so began the development of the gardens with the importation and planting of trees and exotic plants from more temperate climes. Charles Fox's daughter, Juliet, inherited the estate in 1876 and with her husband and Member of Parliament, Edmund Backhouse, continued her father's vision of acquiring hundreds of exotic plants from all over the world, laying out paths and digging pools alongside the stream which ran down the valley. This was the era of the major planting of Rhododendrons.

Following the death of Edmund Backhouse in 1906, Trebah was bought in 1907 by Charles Hawkins Hext and his wife Alice, who despite the death of her husband, continued to develop the garden and the expansion of the plant collection. These were indeed halcyon days for Trebah and perhaps the most famous visitor during Alice's ownership was, in 1935, Edward, Prince of Wales accompanied by Ernest and Wallis Simpson, whose three signatures can be seen in the visitors' book. Prince Edward's letter of thanks to Alice, which also includes thanks for samples of Chatham Island Forget-me-nots for the gardens at Sandringham remains in the Trebah archive.

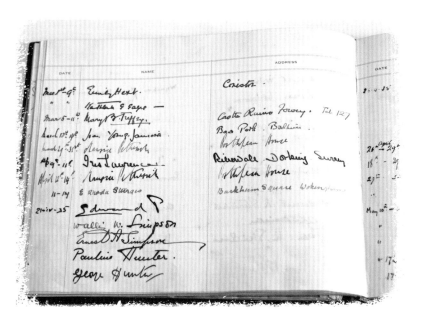

The war years were dark days for Trebah when it was commandeered by the War Office. A military road, still visible, was built to allow access to Polgwiddon Cove which was concreted over to ease movement of military vehicles and tanks on to landing craft. The garden itself was put to use as a storage site for munitions and requisitions and trenches dug in the lower part of the gardens as defence against invasion. It was from Polgwiddon Cove that ten landing craft crammed full with tanks, guns, support vehicles and 7,500 men of the 29th US Infantry Division set sail for Omaha Beach in Normandy via the Isle of Wight on June 1st 1944. A plaque commemorating the officers and men of this assault force has been erected at the bottom of the garden near the beach.

The post-war redevelopment of Trebah back to its original splendour and its further enhancement is due to the great contributions of two families, the Healeys and the Hibberts. Donald Healey, the famous designer of sports cars including the Jensen-Healey and the Austin-Healey, acquired Trebah in 1961 and over the next ten years removed the concrete from Polgwiddon Cove, restored the ponds, built an orchid house and began the huge task of restoring the garden. His memorial plaque is sited at the visitor centre. Over the next ten years, 1971-1980, Trebah changed hands a further twice and during this time suffered significant losses of trees at the hands of severe storms.

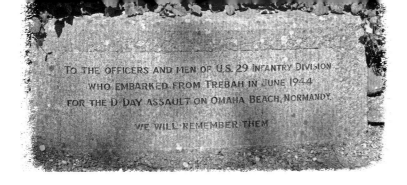

TO THE OFFICERS AND MEN OF U.S. 29 INFANTRY DIVISION
WHO EMBARKED FROM TREBAH IN JUNE 1944
FOR THE D-DAY ASSAULT ON OMAHA BEACH, NORMANDY.

WE WILL REMEMBER THEM

However, in 1981 Major Tony Hibbert, a former paratrooper, and his wife Eira, purchased the estate, initially as a home in which to retire. Not content with simple retirement however, they initiated a programme designed to restore the garden to the status it enjoyed in the 1930s when Trebah was an important part of the horticultural splendour of the UK. The gardens were opened to the public in 1987 to help defray the costs of maintaining them and within two years annual visitor numbers exceeded 36,000. The success of their endeavours can be seen in the beautiful gardens of the present day.

In 1990, The Trebah Garden Trust, a registered charity, took ownership of and responsibility for the management of Trebah Garden and Estate with a mission "to preserve, enhance and recreate the gardens for the education and enjoyment of the public". This included a commitment to raise the awareness of visitors to the scientific issues involved in maintaining and improving the garden and to promote education through artistic endeavour. Such a vision has seen the construction of the Monet-like bridge over Mallard Pond, the water cascade in the Fernery and improvements to the Water Garden. Of particular note is the creation of the semi-circular amphitheatre in the Chilean Coomb as an outdoor performance space, inspired by the Prayer Pits, such as that at Gwennap near Redruth, which were a feature of Methodism in Cornwall. Besides being an obvious place to meet and have a picnic, this inspirational project lends itself to the performance of plays, readings, live music and perhaps, most importantly, to educational talks about the garden, its history and its trees, shrubs, flowers and plants.

The Trust has maintained the tradition of planting new trees, shrubs and bulbs; the Tree Donor Scheme, begun in 2005, encourages friends of Trebah to become part of this tradition by adopting a tree or shrub (70 adopted to date) enabling thereby the introduction of new species and the replacement of trees at the end of their lifespan. Many new benches around the garden are constructed from recycled wood from such trees. Each of these various projects promotes the reputation and award-winning status of Trebah contributing to a legacy for all who will visit in the future. Immerse yourself in its surroundings and enjoy the beauty and atmosphere of this unique place.

David White

The Rockery

From the Top Lawn

April

November

Spring

Autumn

Water Garden

Candelabra Primulas

Rhododendrons

From late March to mid April the whole valley is full of hundreds of Rhododendrons in flower. Many of these date back to the beginning of the 20th century when important introductions of Rhododendrons from the Himalayas were planted at Trebah.

Species such as *R. protistum* from China, the largest of the genus, bears crimson purple flowers, well in advance of the others in February; *R. imberbe* from the central Himalayas at elevations of around 3000m has vivid scarlet flowers; and the leaves of *R. sinogrande* are up to 90cm long and the trusses of creamy yellow flowers are huge.

New collections of big leaved Rhodos have been planted in recent years to ensure future generations will have the benefit of our foresight as we have from our predecessors.

Illustrated is 'Trebah Gem'; bred locally by Richard Gill at his rhododendron nursery in Penryn and planted by head gardener Harry Thomas in 1900; its spring display of large soft pink blooms is a sight to behold.

◄ *R. cyanocarpum*
'Cynthia'

▲ *R. fragrariiflorum*
'Fragrantissimum'

▲ *R. arboreum* var. *roseum*

◄▲ *R.* 'Loderi Pink
Diamond'

▲ *R.* 'Loderi King George'

▲ *R. arboreum* sp.
cinnamomeum

▲ *R. auriculatum*

▲ *R. auriculatum*

▲ *R. campanulatum*

▲ *R. falconeri* ssp. *eximium*

▲▼ *R. falconeri* ssp. *eximium*

▲ *R. edgeworthii*

▲ *R. elegantulum* 'Elizabeth'

▶ *R. coryanum* 'Countess of Haddington'

▲ *R. griersoniunum*

▲ *R. protistum*

▲ *R. maddeni* ssp. maddeni polyandrum

▲ *R. occidentale*

▲ *R. luteum*

◄ *R. lindleyi* 'Dame Edith Sitwell'

▲ *R. protistum* var. giganteum

Late May

The Bamboozle

Dinky's Puddle

Tressie

Davidia involucrata
var. *vilmoriniana*

April

November

Spring

Alice's Seat

Acers – November

Embothrium coccineum – Chilean Fire Bush

Cyclamen coum

Narcissus 'Trebah Gem'

Narcissus 'Eira Hibbert'

Narcissus 'Trebah'

Gunnera Passage

January

Azalea Bank - Spring

Hydrangea Valley

Hydrangea 'Trebah Silver'

Hydrangeas

Approximately two acres of predominantly blue mophead Hydrangeas encircle Mallard Pond. These were planted in the 1950s and the cut blooms were sent to Covent Garden flower market and sold on to London hotels and restaurants.

The plants benefit greatly from the careful hand pruning they receive in early spring each year, and produce abundant flower heads. They are mostly vivid blue due to the rich acid soil at Trebah.

The Hydrangeas flower from around late June and in many mild autumns can still be looking good up to Christmas.

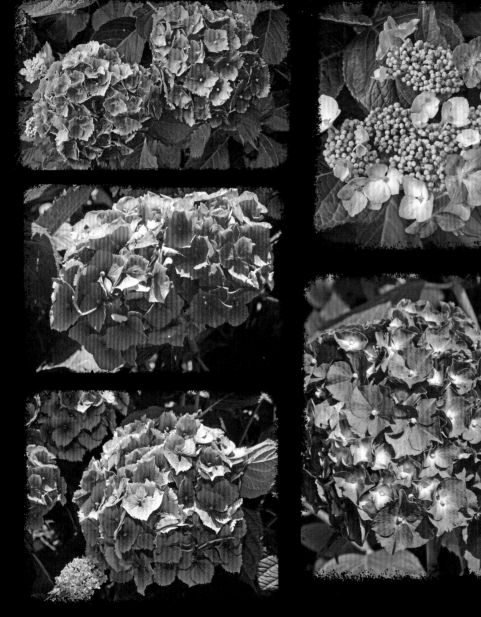

Trebah Beach

Magnolias

Trebah has a collection of over 30 different types of Magnolia; some date back to the turn of the 20th century but many others have been planted since then.

The giant *Magnolia campbellii* (illustrated) from the Himalayas, at the head of the Chilean Coomb is the largest in the UK at 24m and flowers on bare branches in February and makes a tremendous statement in the early spring.

Many beautiful Magnolia species and hybrids including *M. kobus* from Japan with fragrant white flowers, *M. doltsopa* 'Silver Cloud' with big white heavily scented blooms, and *M. x soulangeana*, one of the best and most popular Magnolias for general planting can be enjoyed during the months of March and April.

▲ *M. x brooklynensis* 'Caerhays Surprise'

▲ *M. sieboldii* ssp.*sinensis*

◄ *M. sprengeri* 'Diva'

▶ *M. x brooklynensis* 'Caerhays Surprise'

▲ *M. doltsopa* 'Silver Cloud'

▲ *M. kobus*

▲ *M. x soulangeana*

Trachycarpus fortunei

Sequoia sempervirens

Laureliopsis philippiana

Hedychium coronarium

The Stumpery & Cascade

Late Spring

Autumn

Winter

▲▼ *Puya berteroniana*

▲ *Puya chilensis*

▲ *Puya compacta*

Koi pool

Camellia japonica
'Kings Ransom'

Camellias

Trebah's collection of Camellias enjoys a long flowering period lasting from November through to May. The extensive plantings along Camellia Walk and Petrys Path took place in the 1950s. At Trebah we have over 70 different varieties ranging from deep red (*C.* 'MacDonalds Seedling') to pure white (*C. japonica* 'White Swan') with every shade of pink in between.

Examples of the x williamsii hybrids can be found, such as 'Jenefer Carlyon' with its large open flowers. Other 'specials' to look out for include *C. japonica* 'Guillio Nuccio', rated as one of the finest cultivars ever bred or *C. sasanqua* 'Crimson King' probably one of the oldest Camellias in the garden, which produces vivid scarlet scented flowers before Christmas each year.

▲ *C. x williamsii* 'Jurys Yellow'

▲ *C.* 'MacDonalds Seedling'

▲ *C. x williamsii*

▲ *C. williamsii* 'Glens Orbit'

▲ *C. japonica* 'Adolf Audusson'

▲ *C. japonica* 'C. M. Hovey'

▲ *C. japonica* 'Conspicua'

▲ *C. japonica* 'Hakurakuten'

▲ *C. japonica* 'Giullio Nuccio'

▲ *C. japonica* 'Sacco Nova'

▲ *C. japonica* 'Nuccios Pearl'

▲ *C. japonica* 'Imbricata Rubra'

▲ *C. japonica* 'Saturnia'

▲ *C. japonica* 'Mathoutiana Alba'

▲ *C. japonica* 'Lavinia Maggi'

▲ *C. japonica* 'Nuccios Jewel'

▲ *C. japonica* 'Tomorrow'

▲ *C. reticulata* 'Arch of Triumph'

▲ *C. x williamsii* 'Elegant Beauty'

▲ *C. x williamsii* 'Jenefer Carlyon'

▲ *C. x williamsii* 'Anticipation'

▲ *C. reticulata x williamsii* 'Leonard Messel'

Garden Staff

The present dedicated gardening team of just four people with 67 years of employment at Trebah between them bears testament to the loyalty and enjoyment of working in such a beautiful garden. A continual motivating factor is that of being part of a unique project that is still developing and evolving. In addition to the full-time staff, Trebah is very fortunate in having a small group of keen and supportive volunteer gardeners.

Visitor Centre

The Visitor Centre was opened in 2002 and named in honour of the Hibbert family and in particular Major & Mrs Tony Hibbert who were instrumental in re-developing the Garden and creating the Trust that now runs Trebah.

It comprises two shops and a spacious eating area with outside plant sales. It has added considerably to the experience of visiting Trebah and has made the Garden a round-the-year attraction.